Dented Brown Fedora

by
Gary Beaumier

UnCollected Press

Dented Brown Fedora
Copyright © 2020 by Gary Beaumier

All rights reserved. This book in full form may not be used or reproduced by electronic or mechanical means without permission in writing from the author and UnCollected Press.

Cover Art:
    Phyllis Nasiopulos
    Untitled

Book Design by:

UnCollected Press
8320 Main Street, 2nd Floor
Ellicott City, MD 21043

For more books by UnCollected Press:
www.therawartreview.com

First Edition 2020
ISBN: 9781736009819

Table of Contents
A Church in the Landscape of Thought 1
Bone and Memory 3
Dented Brown Fedora 5
Cold Season 7
The Going Rate 8
Night Train to Paris 10
canticle for an insomniac 12
Buried in the Sky 13
Midnight at the Antiquarian Book Shop 15
Escanaba River 17
Re-imagining My Father 19
The Third to Last Time I Saw Antoine 20
In the End 21
Driving Through North Dakota at Night 23
Ghosting 25
Corporations of Love 26
Hart Island 27
In the Warehouse of Old Souls 30
Into a Darkening Sky 31
Rented Orange Dumpster 33
Speculations On A Lost Shoe 34
Everything's a Gun Now 35
Some Dead Comedian 37
The Northern Lights 39
Becoming Nureyev's Ghost 41
Poetry Busker Of Kathmandu 43
If Night So Too the Morning 45
Kept Things 46
Some Still Come to Ask 48
La Mer 49
Mister Rogers 50
A Better Offering of Light 51
Letting Go 52
Ten Cents 54
Meditating in the Presence of Mice 55

Misshapen Hearts	56
Remembering Your Repeated Attempts at Living	58
Rain	60
Failure to Thrive	62
My Father's Heart as a Timeline	63
The Rio Grande	64
The Spirit of the Horse	66
Three Summer Nights	67
To the Lighthouse	69
Render Me Onto	70
From Certain Distances In Space	72
A Father Walks His Daughter Down the Aisle	74
In the Place Just Before Sleep	76
Night Forest	77
Punch Drunk Shadow Boxing	78
Three Views on the Flight of Geese	80
Upon The Place Beneath	82
Rain to Snow	84
Between the Longing and the Real	86
The Migratory Habits of Dreams in Late Autumn	87
Whistling Rachmaninov	89
The Dimensions of Your Soul	90
Places I Have Known	91
Wordplay with Rock	93
Your Red Hair	95
Another Old Man Full Of Stories	96
Still Life	98
When We Were New	100
Lower Forms of Life	102
On the Second Occasion of His Passing	104
The Complete History of Our First Kiss	105
From My Family to Yours	107
Keeping You Close	108
Last Things	110
Merely Us	112
The Distance to the Moon	113

July 10, 1939 115
Dmitri I Have No Music for This 117
How She Grieved the Old Piano 119
The Way Station 120
Touch 121

To my wife Mary who can recite a remembered Yeats poem that never fails to make me swell with emotion, even after half a lifetime together —

To my son Ben and daughter Mara who nobly negotiate this ever more perilous world —

To Phyllis Nasiopulos for her lovely cover art —

And finally to my own mother and father, Verna and Lawrence, gone these many years now, though I still carry the memories of them, the bitter and the sweet —

A Church in the Landscape of Thought

I am fluent in the language of memory

conversant with the dead
a companion of ghosts

sometimes a penitent to my regrets
mea culpa,
          mea culpa

sometimes a vertigo of dreads

a captive to introspections

… until my dog dances joyous
as he bursts onto virgin snow
snow that mutes the darkening eve

 then my thoughts yield to poplars and oaks
— branches blessed in white—
punctuated by crooked fencing
and toppling outbuildings
a rusted tractor stranded in the field beyond
while one owl calls
in vespers
as another answers
and a procession of deer
cross along the far rise
backlit in moonlight
Ave Maria
Ave Maria

such a holy thing to lose your mind
to Sunday quiet
may it hold me a minute more
may it keep me forever

Bone and Memory

One of the last soldiers
of the Great War
—little more than
bone and memory—
prays to his late wife-
because his
God was a casualty
of the trenches.

He yet feels the sweep
of her hand
on his shoulders
when,
between dreams,
she checked for him
in their bed
to assure herself
that he really
returned to her

... and she settled him
from night terrors
gathering him to her body
The screams of artillery shells
And dying men

(Men hold so stoic a pose
until they shatter
completely)

His milky eyes
and damaged ears
have let his mind
mingle the past and present
so that to him
she is still beside him
while his lips move
to beseech her
with a lover's catechism.

"Give me the mercy
of your touch
the solace of your breath
into my breath
the caress of your voice
that I may dwell
In the safety that is you"

Finally, a nurse
presses a straw to his lips
as 11:11
marches across
the face of the clock.

Soon the war will be over.

Dented Brown Fedora

My father,
all his days,
was tracked
by a wolf
three paces behind;
he'd warn me of this blood beast.
Then one day
late into his years
that wolf ate my father's heart.

There were days
though
when the wolf fell behind.
I knew this was so
when my father would sing the old songs
in a crooner's voice
as he readied himself
for his day.
Or in the evening
when he'd relight his cigar stub,
slick with spit,
and work through a quart of beer
that would cast an amber light
on the kitchen table.

In the summer now
I rise early to run
before the sun breaks over the water
and my father keeps pace,
working through my thoughts.
There are different sounds in this rural place --
birds call in their easy glide --
but I hear his raspy breath
overlapping mine,
and for all my days
I'm kept in the company
of a ghost and a beast.

Not far into the run
my body yields
to a slipstream of motion
outpacing the voices
and the dread
and all my self-inflicted thoughts —
if for just for a moment —

and even as he recedes from me
I see him in his dented brown fedora
cigar in his teeth
as he watches my graceful stride
and maybe he's saying,
"You keep this moment, son, as long as you can."

Cold Season

The snowmelt unburied the carnage
from the cold season
willow ash and maple's stripped branches
soaked in winter's blood
crooked themselves beseechingly
for a little more of the sun's nourishment

There were such hobgoblins
in the winter's nights
nibbling at the edges of thought
such catastrophes of the body that
I nurtured a wish to simply
be torn away in my sleep
in a strong gust of dreams
--one breath then no more—
and scattered amongst others I'd known

but now I rise at first light
to put to fire the conquered bones in the garden
letting the burning scents mingle
in my hair and wools
and when I return to you
you bend to kiss the top of my head
inhaling a smoky aroma
and then wipe a smudge of ash from my forehead

The Going Rate

With his days in short supply
he ventured to this far shrine
I think there must have been a gift shop
with little resin statues of Mary
for which he paid the going rate
then he fell to his knees and prayed
for transcendence

I walk a road I think he motored
but I worship something unknown to me
that comes in first light

long ago I knelt with him
by the couch murmuring,
"Hail Mary Holy Mary"
ten times and ten times and ten times
--unstrung you can follow
the beads back generations--
it was thought to be the going rate

all those promises made with
the pageantry of bright vestments
the heady waft of incense
the reverberations of Latin incantations
off marble walls…
had such assuredness

except I am infected by doubt
except now I think the sun turns indifferently
morning comes like a stained glass window
and a woman tells me God is the best artist
I want to ask her if *belief* is the going rate

yet sometimes still a steeple will catch my eye
to exact its due
so I wonder if I should tender another prayer

my father has gone to Medjugorji

…and you are gone dad
I wish you a kind and soft deliverance
into the arms of your mother
your Mary…
and your God

Night Train to Paris

Our aged bodies
surrender to the sway
and lurch of the train
as we have passed through
the long tunnel
beneath the sea

old is a foreign country
we ride to

when we get there
we will rise to higher places
sit with gargoyles
balance on high slate roofs
as light slips through us
we sleep on park benches
dry leaves chasing around
us like wicked urchins

I will fish the river
in a floppy hat
mouthing a Gauloises
and you with a book splayed
in your lap will feed pigeons the remains
of your bread while sitting
on a soft blanket
and we will glance at each other
as only such longtime companions can with a pure knowing

later we will write postcards
from an empty bistro
—trumpet notes weave into the cool dark air—
telling the children back home
we are here now
and they will not see us again

canticle for an insomniac

damn the peaked moon
whose brightness pulls you out of sleep

to hell with bills yet unpaid

such worrisome things to unquiet you

curse the pain in your overburdened shoulders

let the rich man in the limo kiss your ass

horseshoe the pillow around your head
to mute the other's snoring

too late for a sleeping pill to mass murder unruly thoughts

to hell with every ad that promises a trip to *happy*

banish that sun to back to blackness
another day ruined before it starts

...just hold the diamond brilliance of your anger
...just wear your care worn face all the day
—smiles are for liars—

and then let a quiet come to you...
if it will

Buried in the Sky

There are snowflakes
in the early 1940s
There are snowflakes
in the summer
in the camp
you brush one from your shoulder
you will never know
if it was an arm
or face
or a man
or woman
you must remember
how that snowflake
alighted on you
soundlessly

Years later
half a world away
you leave them in your hair
—snowflakes—
on your overcoat
their mentholated cool
on your cheek

Midnight your dreams
bring you to the catwalk
atop the smokestack
of the power plant
Dark shapes

issue from there
the great procession
of humanity
released into the cool
twinkling night
their souls are light as--

A survivor's memory is lead
and stone
and the snowflakes
so very much
weigh you down

These days you straddle
this world
and the other
you could so easily
have been flakes of ash
carried on hot currents of air
out of a tall stack.

Midnight at the Antiquarian Book Shop

"I was most grievously undone
when I lost my footing on the shelf
and swan dived to the floor
splayed and back broken,"
says the complete works of Shakespeare
who now leans against the cash register

"We are— so many of us— a musty assemblage of
    forgotten words.
Trees pressed into paper to hold our messages.
Conceived by some dreamy word dabbler long gone.
Escorting the appreciative few from womb to tomb
Yet now shorn of dust jacket
now a deterioration of spine
dog eared pages and torn scripts
Are we soon to be consigned to a burn pile?"
The selected poetry of Elizabeth Barrett Browning flutters
    her pages
"Slings and arrows, Will," she says woefully, "slings and
    arrows"

"One for all" rallies
a volume of the stories of Dumas

"Ours is not to reason why," says Tennyson on the third
    shelf in 19th century literature

"Still the bespectacled girl comes by after school
And slips a kind hand around me,"
asserts a copy of *Wind in the Willows*.
"Loses herself in my illustrations, she does.
Toad and Badger still wing her imagination."

"I'm hitting the road," says a copy of Kerouac's complete
   works.

"Where you going to go Jack?" asks Alan Ginsburg,
   caressing his cover lovingly.
      "The doors are all locked."
An old dog escapes from Herriot's work
and nuzzles the bard.

"Read to us, William,
in your stentorian voice,"
they all plead
"Read us through the night.
We still love you."

…and so he begins *A Midsummer Night's Dream*
while the other volumes nod approvingly.

Escanaba River

In dreams my father skates
the Escanaba River.
The ice hard frozen and dusted
with snow that swirls
ghostly behind him
as he flies breakneck
toward a sundown
that sets the pine and birch on fire.
He's lean in that way teens are,
tugging his hat over
a thicket of black hair --
earflaps up, daring the cold.
Blades bite the ice as he sways

into a rhythm of greater speed
until he pivots and backward
glides in a lazy "S".

This was his glory!

There are days when
I superimpose myself in this past --
momentarily I become the lord of time,
the curator of some
cataract memory –
and there he is,
largely unformed,
neither father nor husband.

As I meet him this way,
our checkered

relationship and
estrangement
is yet to be.
So we walk companionably
to my grandparents'
past yellow windows,
cheeks and noses red and numb
and tightened from the frozen air.

Re-imagining My Father

I hear my mother's weeping

Some days it catches me up mid sentence
and I cock an ear to its rasping protests

Her torn little phrases spit out
on gusts of emotion

and in some firing of memory
I see a boy in bed not sleeping

who was thinking about his birthday
the next day

until his father accused her
of being with another

Was this some crooked version
of love?

...his intense need of her?

and why do I want to rephrase this for him
so many years later

so he says something softer like:

"I'm so afraid of losing you
to someone else.
Please don't ever leave me."

Yet other days I hear my father's anger inside my words

The Third to Last Time I Saw Antoine

The third to last time I saw Antoine
we walked a city block
after someone threw an insult about his mother
who abandoned him early on
I watched as a tear
rolled down his brown cheek and
I could see the loss was already built into his face.

The second to last time I saw Antoine
he was handcuffed
in the back of a police cruiser
trying to kick out the back window
won over by his molten anger

The last time I saw Antoine
he came to my classroom
to say good bye
so I hugged him
and told him I loved him
and it was the easiest thing
I ever did.

In the End

How I wanted an effortless day
of sailing with you.

But waters can make you confessional
and as the boat heeled from the wind you huddled yourself
in the warm sun against the cabin and said,
"So many drowned beneath us.
Mothers trying to save their babies from sinking ships."

A darkening flock of cormorants flew overhead
while I eased off the sails.

"My father told me I killed my mother while she was
giving me birth," you said.
Clouds pressed in and the whole of the sky wore this crime.

In the end,
in the galleried halls of your memory,
are there only tragic seascapes?
Do you gasp for air
and is this what made you?

 "In the end on his deathbed I told my father I loved him,"
you said after a long pause.
You brightened now and kissed my cheek
while the boat livened to a freshening of wind.

"How could you find it in yourself to say that to him?" I
asked.

"There are days when I'm still a murderer
and there are days when I forgive
and days when I remember that
he lost his wife too," you replied.

In the end you try to make your peace.

Driving Through North Dakota at Night

In the hospital room
I hold my brother's hand.
Hearing is the last thing to go,
so I talk.
"Long ago we drove through
North Dakota all night," I say,
"and just to stay alert you taught me the
names of the '57 Braves:
Spahn and Aaron and Crandall.
It was so dark
I started to see things
on the road ahead,
things that weren't really there.

"Let's drive again,
you and me,
when you're better.
We'll find another '61 Chevy.
No seat belts.
I'll drive while
you find stations on the radio.
Maybe this time
you'll see things
in the darkness.
Maybe you'll
hallucinate God."

But when the nurse comes in,
I know he has crossed into Canada
without me.

Ghosting

The aircraft lights wink behind the copse
of dying ash in the moments shy of dawn
soon the trees will tumble down
one and then another
to give a little more horizon
and who could know in the plane
that somewhere in their distance I watch

I have walked the long night
on the road by the sea
where lights are all that define the ships
plying the phosphorescent waves
but I don't know why

and I don't know how I became this…
at first I thought it was just a dreaming
or light-headedness
but maybe I am
little more than a slip of smoke
from a guttered candle taken on a current of air
its afterimage held in the few memories of others

that my footfalls make no sound now…
that you passed me in the hallway this evening
and took no notice…

…and yet I follow a silvering of light
escaping beneath the bedroom door
(you have assumed some of my side of the bed now)
as I have come to remember
you are still my destination
and maybe you will lift your head
and say my name

Corporations of Love

It is no small tragedy to learn
your car is not made of love;
to know you will not achieve
blissful sleep
and wake in a delirium of
happiness,
all because your mattress
won't fit your contours;

to think that pill won't restore
some version of peace.

Should I hug my empty places?

Should I dance an awkward step
with the industries of joy?

Should we run into the flow of traffic
hands held in a pact?

Or shall I kiss you all the night
and rename *love* in secret?

Hart Island

When I was seven
I'd lie in the autumn grass
and pretend to be dead,
my hands clasped solemnly,
like when they laid out my grandfather,
inhaling the scent of burning leaves,
as light and dark danced over my face.
Family and friends wept over me
and, because I was seven,
I could hear them
and I could play with death so easily.

On a slip of an island off New York
they number the trenches
where they stack the unclaimed
three deep,
a million and counting.
Riker's inmates,
with infinite tenderness,
lower babies
who lived only short minutes
after birth.
Mothers who sign
for a city burial
never know they'll have no plot
to grieve over.

Maybe the strains of Saint-Saens
will waft over this subterranean world

hand reanimate
the estranged,
the anonymous,
into some ghastly carnival of dance.

Far into the night
a shard of moonlight
cuts across my pillow
to steal my sleep.
I zombie walk my old body
with blankets and flask
to the bed of our rusted pickup.
The moon playfully sails
behind a thick meringue
of clouds
as I compose myself
and surrender
to the variations of darkness
and dream of a million
untended souls.

In a rum-addled stupor
I awaken to an apparition
performing a curious dance
--until I realize it's my love
come to claim me.

"Watch the night with me

a little longer," I beg

and then ask her
if she needs a place
to grieve over
should I be the first
...but she just shakes her head
in a way I know to mean
"You crazy old man"
and kisses my cheek.

In the Warehouse of Old Souls

"I love the smell of urine in the morning,"
the man next to me says
to tweak the movie line.
After breakfast, the aides wheel us in front of the television.
In two minutes I'm asleep,
head bowed to my chest,
but my dreams take me to the moon.
Gravity is kinder here
as I bound over craters
and kick up dust.
I shout down to my fellow residents,
"Hey you got to try this,"
and leap 20 feet in the air.
Later I walk to the dark side
and snuggle into a crater,
thrilled by the firmament all freckled in planets and stars.
When they wheel my hulk
to the lunch table,
they'll think I'm just sleeping.

Into a Darkening Sky

The farmer parted the tall grass with a stick
to reveal asparagus growing in the rocks
to his young sons
rocks collected by generations of farmers
partitioning the fields.

The grey tossed his head
as she cinched the girth on the saddle;
so full of himself.
She upended a milking pail
to mount keeping a leg on him
to check his eagerness
as she rode him past the garden.

Then she eased the reins
to let him find his pace.
He lengthened
and she could feel the power
in his flanks as he gained speed.
He could throw her now,
smash her head against the rocks
and a week later nothing but a green phallus
to mark the spot,
and that too would go to seed.

As she flew past her husband and children
she turned a look of one possessed on them
and they did not know this wife and mother.

On she went her let-out hair streaming
like the grey's tail flowing back and away;
away like the land that ties her;
away like the depression she felt after each birth;
away like the disappointments in her marriage
But now she moved in rhythm
with her young lover beneath her
and she could steal away, west to the big river
and into a darkening sky.

Rented Orange Dumpster

We launched the memory-saturated
contents of your parents'

home arching kitsch and artifact over the side
of the battered orange

dumpster. This is why they push the bones
to the back of the crypts in

New Orleans. We heave a piss stained mattress
that carried the last of your father's

dreams…lifeless and awkward.
I gather you to me and kiss your

sweated brow *Will it be this way for us?*
a thought I keep to myself-- *solemn and*

irreverent both--children cursing our
accumulations ask "Why

did they even keep this?" They will be
the custodians of faulty

memories that have come
unattached to the things we

kept while our bones separate as we are
pushed to the back

we must be gotten out of the way too.

Speculations On A Lost Shoe

Three days running I've noticed a woman's sandal
set out on a picnic table near the beach waiting to be
reclaimed

I imagine its owner walking the shore
steadying herself on her lover's arm
after the last notes of the blues fest
carried over the late summers waters
as she tucked her footwear in her handbag
and let her painted toes ooze sand between each
until that left one tumbled out
and was cruelly taken by the lake

And later still
when she found it missing
she asked herself wistfully
"Is this the price of love?"

Everything's a Gun Now

At the bar where he got shot
I was in the line of fire

The three year old
at the food store
holds a banana
like a pistol

"One Killed in Bar Brawl"
the headlines said
Can you be wounded and not shot,
I ask

people laugh in rapid fire
rat a tat tat

One man threatened
with a cue stick
the other
pushed a gun
into the soft of his belly

I've got the thousand yard stare until
the car with the broken muffler
sounded like a gun

He doubled over
after a mute report

a middle finger
can blow my head off

Face gone cardboard grey

It is writ holy
that you're a militia
of one

life ebbed into a blood puddle

The double-barreled guy
on the radio
turns words to bullets --
Eventually, I'll get what's
coming to me, he says.

Some Dead Comedian

After we separated
I rescued a dog from the animal shelter
and named him Gus
he was a terrier mix and would kill
rabbits and squirrels

once when he ran away I
knew I had to find him or die trying

after we separated I brought offerings of chrysanthemums
and coffee to your doorstep and then wondered
if you'd throw them out and
I'd walk away feeling pathetic

with my Airstream in tow
Gus and I drove the country
we were a little bit Steinbeck and a little bit Charlie
as I autopsied our relationship
but even vast prairies or wide rivers
couldn't help me figure it out.

so when my money ran low
and I returned and you found me
one evening when the sun had dropped
you held Gus like you knew him forever
and thanked me for the flowers

you said it wasn't my fault

but that you always broke things

and you didn't know why

then you quoted some dead comedian
"I don't want to belong to any club
that will accept me as a member.
I guess that was true of us too," you said.

The Northern Lights

I never took your last breath;
you never saw my first.
So when I was young
I invented fathers
to take your place,
television dads;
doting dispensers of wisdom
smelling of aftershave
and martinis.
I refused to learn to ride a bike,
certain you'd come along eventually
and teach me how.
Other times you shadowed me,
unable to reveal yourself
due to secret government work
but you'd save me in some moment of peril
at the last second,
only to vanish again.

By high school
Norman Rockwell was the cruelest man I knew with all his
paintings of normal.
And I hated everyone
who went on about how stupid their father was
"Try not having one," I'd think.

Finally when I was sixty
I bought an old truck
and drove deep into Canada
where I knew you last were.

It broke down twice
but, even though I could never fix
my bad marriages, I could fix trucks.

I was not ready
for the aurora
to back light the cemetery
where I stumbled around
and found your untended stone.
I was three beers into my night
and about to read a letter I wrote to you
where every sentence began with "why"
when something in me just let go
and I quietly whispered
"thank you dad"
and turned back to leave it all behind.

Becoming Nureyev's Ghost

The slip of a girl who works in the coffee shop
seems to define the very space around her
all suppleness and grace and lightness is she

The conversation sputters and falters
as my friend and I both rush to save ourselves
from the silent places that fall between
our chatter until I lose myself in a lull
and

suddenly I rise up.
I am Nureyev's ghost
she, this barista, is Fonteyn and
our gazes lock

I feel my body collect itself
I'm on point
hands on hips like a matador

We execute soaring leaps
over tables and chairs
gliding past each other in midair
then I catch her and she bends
easily in my supporting arm
I raise her above my head
her lithe body almost lifts itself
arms upward legs tucked
we are fluid in perfect sync

Just as quickly I return to my table
make my excuses to my friend
and fumble for my cane
I nearly topple over a chair

as I head to the door a little mortified
I glance back once and mutter, "ah Margot
how you quicken this heart"

...but she only calls
out to the person
who ordered
a cappuccino

Poetry Busker Of Kathmandu

I think I could be a poetry busker
in the London tube.
I'd pilfer library books;
kept in a paper grocery sack
and do recitations
to busy commuters
who'd would likely
take no notice of me
"Do you see what a metaphor
you are for your life
hurriedly going nowhere?"
I'd say.
But
someone could stop;
listen.
When I'd finish
I'd tear the poem out of the book
"Here,
this is yours now.
Say it again and again
out loud.
Bring it into your sleep.
Find the cadence.
Hear how it resonates in your morning shower;
how it finds your sadness,
your loss
your anger
your joy.

Mostly though
I think I'm a busker
on the streets of Kathmandu
speaking English as
crowds go by
a foreign face,
foreign tongue.
"The barbarian makes curious sounds like tiny hammers
striking something dissonant,"
they would say.

Would they eventually adopt me,
this street corner reader?
Pitch a coin in my satchel?
Here's a page.
Here's a page.

If Night So Too the Morning

Did you know I whisper things to you
in the night when you are seized in a paralytic sleep
we are night's conquest in its negligee of fog
night that mimics our finality

Did we defy mortality long ago
with our little deaths
our delicious agonized finishes

I hover my face over you
to match my breathing to yours
and wonder of the course and variance
of your dreams as I whisper

let them commingle --these dreams--
in some recitation of our infirmities
--a weakness here a breakage acknowledged--
this is how night works its murderous ways

we are now with badly mended wings
but I will fly these hours with you
to where night takes us as its downdrafts
smash us to the ground

I whisper regrets with a crumpled face
I whisper love with ashen breath
I whisper lust with a kiss to you hand
and even as the grey dawn creeps
beyond the shuttered windows
and everything is stripped away

It is then we find ourselves new
and perfect again.

Kept Things

Dad was a hoarder
child of the great depression
keeper of little things
non-dairy creamer
pouches of sugar
secreted in pockets
tucked in the back of drawers

During his fights
with my mother
he'd reach back in his memory
and take out his grievances
"Unfair" my mother would say
"to bring up something
that happened so long ago"

…until one day he bloodied
the kitchen with
a catsup packet he burst
on the counter
and replied to
her, "but I'm still hurt
after all these years."

Later my mother brought
him his dinner
while he hid behind
his newspaper nurturing
his wounds
and an uneasy peace would
last for several days

Some Still Come to Ask

I should have been a student of the sky
to watch squadrons of geese make passage
beneath low autumn clouds.
Stars could lift my heart as I hold forth with
astronomical terms like "nebula" or "quasar"
and,
while in a hammock,
held in broad trees, I'll know
branches are emissaries
to other realms,
where the moons overpower reason.

I could acquaint myself
with the retired
who fish along the quay
and see their days in total
and find their peace
in the lap and lull of the water,
speaking just to quietly ask
"Are they biting today?"

I should have studied
 the nomenclature of the old
and listened to their lamentations
--- bad hearts and sad memories --
just to know that some still come to ask,
"Was this not heaven?"

La Mer

It is the reach and sweep
of the horizon
that seduces the eye
the darker folds of clouds
the insinuation
of rose just above the water
a breeze moist and warm
like the touch of first love

a boat secured
to the outermost mooring
rocks an afternoon away
a little wine
a book
and the plink of
piano notes
from the classical station
that escape
the raucous
confusion of gulls
while a wave geysers upward
high as the lighthouse

Mister Rogers

When my mother moved
to a high rise retirement home
we'd sit on the open air balcony
of the 20th floor and look over the city
and amidst the panorama of
cars and trucks flowing along the interchange
or office complexes next to
little patches of green parks
my mother, fragile as autumn leaves,
would offer short reminisces
of her life tinged with a regret… I'd heard it all before.

Some mornings when I visited
I'd find her watching Mister Rogers
while smoking a cigarette and I'd sit next to her
and she'd give me her hand in greeting
keeping her eyes on the TV.

Finally when a stroke took her voice away.
Her well kept hair became a nest of tangles.
I rubbed oil into her hands and feet and face
And brushed her hair very carefully
And said you let go when you're ready ma
I know I was loved by you
and there isn't anything truer then that
But in the end there was just the uneven breathing

…and I do not think she heard.

A Better Offering of Light

You know it's cold
when you wake because
you can see the stars
just like you know earlier
there was a new snow
since there is a sharper glow
in the middle distance
as you look out the window
and wonder
are the willow branches
a little more finely etched
in a better offering of light?

you dress in the dark
his voice rises from the blankets
the lilt of his words skips
to remembered verse
"When you are old and grey
and full of sleep…"
his breath a little rank
as your lips find his forehead
and how did you know
he really meant
he loves you?

later you hum
a soothing tune
as you make his coffee
and how will he know
you really meant that too?

Letting Go

Write a poem,
Build a boat.

Find one that pleases your eye
that will carry you
lively across the water
on a summer's day

bend the oak for framing
plank her in a white cedar
deep grains for her breast hooks

Worry your fingers
over each plank
as you fair her
and give her a color
-blue or green-
and a pleasing name

Then tie off her tiller
 set her sail
push her off
without you

maybe she'll find
a tired swimmer
who'll hoist himself aboard
and let her carry him a while.

Build a boat,
Write a poem.

Ten Cents

Once
I saw a man,
whose brother
had been murdered,
sidearm a coin
into a fountain
and for years
I puzzled
over what this meant.

In the time
that followed
was the cheap prattle,
of weather speculations,
and baseball scores,
while his heartbeat kept time to some
inner dirge
that held him at a remove
and his countenance only broke open once –
as he sailed the life of his brother
on a dime
into the water.

Meditating in the Presence of Mice

No equanimity here
when they cross the top
of my feet,
crawl up my pant leg
and pause for a moment
on my lap
(Deep breath
mind blank)
Yet another crawls into my head.
Ones I thought I banished
years ago skitter back.

Regrets, embarrassments, old wounds --
Old age has many such
infestations of memory.

Misshapen Hearts

It's 11 pm at the memory buffet
all my friends gone to shadows
and my children
scattered like autumn geese
and me
living past my time

I wonder if the man who calculated
the actuary table has died
and I chuckle to think
he might have looked
at his watch
just before he expired
and said,
"Yup, right on time"

It's 11 pm at this third rate
nursing home
and Marie comes in my room.
She is small and thin and has
two fingers missing on her left hand
but when she helps me with
my pills she is disarmingly patient
for which I'm more grateful
then she could know

"I love you Marie," I say
and in reply she smoothes back
my hair and says,

"Go to sleep now,"
because she doesn't believe
love should be this way.

Remembering Your Repeated Attempts at Living

Looking back now
you should have been admired
for dodging cars in downtown traffic
wishing to be broken
against chrome and steel

...congratulated for
for confessing to the cashier
at the drugstore
that you were in a
state of grievous sin
(though your transgressions
could have only been slight)...

...applauded for trying
to jump from a moving automobile,
opening the door to a press
of air and blur of pavement,
because the world spun
too fast for you

...and cheered when you shuffled the halls
of the psychiatric unit
nearly insensible from thorazine...

But no one heard the
desperate eloquence
of your gestures, your attempts

Life blessed you
with its curses
and by the time
you mouthed the shotgun
that burst your eyes from their sockets
those eyes weren't seeing much
anymore
anyway...

or maybe they were
looking toward
your next incarnation

Rain

This house is worn
and comfortable and I know
its music
the furnace igniting
the sigh of the wind in the gable
the snare drum rattle of window pane
it is an old friend as I listen to
the hush of a brother's breathing near

Down the hall
the conversational
patter of my mother
and dad as they bed
for the night
and the sounds
of when they take to each other
like a much needed rain

Years since when
my life parched
I've stolen a late evenings
walk past that house
we still know each other
that place and I
as I search through
windows for memories kept
—the world and sky about to break—
and I think
you were much needed rain

and down the lane
where they have bedded
in the ground
—mother and father—
no more whisperings
in the night
as I stand over them
simply to abide my longing

Failure to Thrive

This road is remembered
like a young river,
switchbacks and oxbows,
and your bare feet on the dash
while you nursed a Pabst,
tranced by the wood and
field whirring by,
as my battered car
swayed through another bend
and chased a sundown up one more hill
until we climbed a lookout tower
and you sat on the rail
one hundred feet up.
I should have known then
that one day you'd let yourself fall.

Now this old river runs pretty straight
and in the half light of a winter's eve
a lone doe crosses the ice.
I think she means to remind me of something,
but I'm long practiced in the art of forgetting.

My Father's Heart as a Timeline

When the doctor opened your chest
for the second time
your heart had gone along
unceasingly for 81 years

Long ago there was a beat
for the start of a war.
And one for the man who
first crossed the Atlantic
in his airplane.
A beat for financial doom.
A louder beat for your first born.
A quieter one for me.

Then they became less
decisive.
Beats became flutterings;
once a heart
now a bird
that took flight
conveying your soul
elsewhere.
Though I have no idea
as to the whereabouts of
this elsewhere.

The Rio Grande

After you ran
to that godforsaken border town
I took a plane to find you.

In a blizzard
they deiced the wings
again and again
as I gave in to sleep
imagining I could still hear the
"tock tock" of your heart monitor
before you were born
--like footfalls down a corridor--
predicting all the steps you'd
take in life
but
it didn't predict this.
All the while the jet struggled upwards;
driving snow traded for a harsh blue sky.

When I came upon you my boy,
I resisted holding
you in my arms
for a long moment
sensing it would give you no comfort.
So the best I could do was
leave you broken
and coax you back home
where you might be fixed
by others who were damaged,

even though to be broken
has a beauty all its own
that someday
you may put your arms around.

The Spirit of the Horse

There are deep impressions in the grass,
tracks from your truck and muddied sod
from the vet who "put him down"
and finally from the renderer
who took his lifeless mass away.

Once he took flight in the pasture
throwing up clods of earth.
All that power and grace
so easily extinguished.

On some morning after the last turn
in your sleep you may hear a
whinny or a nicker and not know
if his spirit visits.
And all the longing for him
divines into this unguarded
moment or in the stillness
of a snowscape a moon set
will throw a shadow and that shadow
will be a horse.
and should you run
out to the new snow
and find it hoof pocked
it is all because their living
and their passing pressed so deeply
on your mind and in your soul.

Three Summer Nights

In Edinburgh once
I hopped a moving trolley
easy as a smile.
I hung on the hand rail
and lit an English Oval
spit a fleck of tobacco
into the cool of the summer air
and let it ride me
where it would
bumping along
through the night.

On Saint Finbar's road
there's a little cemetery
halfway to nowhere
where I loved you
beer and blanket
our bare backs
against the cool of a headstone
we were moving objects
briefly intersected
in the moonless dark
You were shadows and Braille
to me as I read your body
with lips and fingers.

Against a star flooded sky
a satellite passes made of
old trolley parts

the earth turns east
I'm porous with moonlight
Let a thousand birds
convey me to that
object in the upper strata;
the merest of distances.

To the Lighthouse

The sun bounces off the water
waves toss jagged glints of light
as they break into a shrapnel of drops
against the limestone

the sea has punished the concrete fortification
leading to the lighthouse as a couple dance step
around tricky footing she takes his arm
scrimshawed with tattoo

you must not know the arch of your years to come
as you stand beneath the shadow of this structure
wrapped around each other
ready to laugh off any battering

maybe just know you'll both be a light to the other

and that you must dance a little when you can

even near the killing sea

Render Me Onto

When I am turned to ash
sprinkle me on the
back of a cormorant
that I make migrate to a warmer clime

Shake me salty
on robins' eggs
blue as the sky
and see me come spring

Sift my grit between your fingers
and toss me skyward
into a gust of south wind

Dust me on each corner of
our home that I may stay with
you a little longer

As for my recalcitrant parts
the ones you found so difficult in me
give them to the sea
and task it with my softening
to take as an apology
for my living days

Rub a little on the back
of your brown horse
brown as your eyes
so we may ride
a trail to no particular place

Spread a little of me in the paddock
fence posts crooked

from winter's heaving

Take care that the breeze
doesn't toss me back
to flour
your face like a baker
lingering like a kiss there

**From Certain Distances In Space
I Still See My Brother**

Somewhere mother holds you against her breasts in
a Chicago flat
-- the war winding down --
while she warms a bottle and tests the milk on the
tender of her wrist;
"you are my sunshine," she sings.

Somewhere you sit in a quilted coat
upon a tricycle in front of a red house,
and later still your fastball hisses over
home plate into the strike zone.

Somewhere a man says we all derive from stars,
while a holy person declares we will live forever.

You still succor your fractious babies as you pace a
midnight floor.

Only just now a distant planet watches you bend to
help a student
or soften your embrace to your wife in the utter
dark.

Somehow you glide out of a fifth floor hospital
room into a painted twilight,
into streams of cars and trucks and exhaust
as your family holds your emancipated body and
rides with you to the edge of life

and somewhere a medical student
peels back what remains of you
to learn the human clockwork

A Father Walks His Daughter Down the Aisle and Gives Her Away

Some mornings the soft caress of sleep lingers
as my mind straddles the millennia
only to remember a Buddhist monk
who self immolated in protest on a Saigon Street.
and the Zupruder film starring JFK
or the Viet Kong
caught by the photographer
the instant of the shot
-- that eternal wince --
all carried into the start
of another thousand years

There are mornings when I sit
and burn in some pandemonium
my mind a scattershot of thought
until it alights upon watching her
watch the world from two and a half feet
back when she straddled my hip
and locked her sticky fingers around my neck
and that will still happen when
she takes a lover or swears an oath to marriage
just as my father carried me down the hall half asleep
and he carries me still
as one moment carries another.

So may she heft the violence of her words
and know how they become lodged in another

and let her curse me
that she was not readied for this
and curse again that I carried her too long
or not long enough
may her struggles with this man
dissolve into tenderness
and may the press of his lips,
sweet upon her forehead,
gentle the last of her thoughts.

In the Place Just Before Sleep

After she bequeathed you a teapot
she rode the jet stream to a distant land.
Do you recall?

Old memories disconnect in the upper strata
unaffected by the tug of the planet
until they return to you
in the place just before sleep
and you free fall back to consciousness
one last time as you catch them.

In the morning you linger
in the amniotic wash of the shower.
aged body savaged by the exertions of gravity,
and you wail an old ballad against the acoustics
of the tiles as the memories cascade
until the one that takes you back to tea.

In that pot a steep of chamomile's vapor and
particles of the yellow flower loosed in the warm
    brew
made ceremoniously and sweetened
to her liking and then

the touch from cautious and tentative
to furious in short moments
with the bold unlayering
of wools and cottons;
surrendered to one another, by turns,
and finally her name in your head streaming
to this very moment to your last moment
to be the last thing you will know.

Night Forest

Once there was a woman in the night forest
who could hear above the register of most.
She would listen to mice sing in chorus
or coyotes comfort their young
over the flash and rumble of coming weather.

There was the night when I stayed in the garden
late into the hours and you called for me
and together we watched the gods
toss stars across the sky and later
we returned to our bed and I watched you
over the vastness of our pillows
as your breathing fell into a rhythm
and you separated from me.

Have your dreams returned you to a wooded place,
dusted in moonlight, where you keen your ears
to other selves, selves beyond the register of my
knowing?

Punch Drunk Shadow Boxing

Did you not know
that even our unsavory features
can be a dark and holy place

We land such punches
upper cuts
to ourselves
and for what?

I knew you when
you'd censor yourself
words that only just escaped
your mouth you'd
gather back
like tiny orphans

and who am I to talk?
I've wished myself away
all too often

by what measure do
we come to such
metastasized thoughts
phrases that infect our introspections

we have combed our hair
and rehearsed our lines
still they glance

at the darker shapes
the light throws against the wall.

still we wave
at the unblemished
and say
"look here at all my shiny things."

Three Views on the Flight of Geese

I
It is gravity we aged fight
Its greedy hands tugging us
down and down.
Through the window
I watch the geese
startled into flight
by wind gusts
while a mother
holds her child
(Red suit against the snowscape)
as the child watches
then flies too…

II
My little pink daughter
throws her arms upward
to aid their assent
and fly with them.
I tighten my hold
around this purely loved
and sync my wonderment
with hers.
Not yet my sweetheart;
don't fly away yet…

III
We three take the wind,
whoosh,

as the earth spins

and falls away.
We search again
for a bare, unsnowed
patch of grass to crop.
Riding a thermal to a new place
While migrating another soul.
Our wings bank toward a landing;
one, two, three.

Upon The Place Beneath

During an intense shelling
I heard
the sergeant recite:
"The quality of mercy
is not strained.
It droppeth as a gentle rain…"
until he took a direct hit
and the pages
of Shakespeare
fluttered down like a dove
blown out of the sky

Given a half a chance
they will bayonet the
Mona Lisa,
crush her smile into
the mud and rubble —
pulverize Venus de Milo
Into pebbles and dust
or machine gun
Van Gogh's quiet bedroom,
the canvas holed beyond
any recognition.

So
we obliterated their
concert halls with our aerial bombs,
pianos turned to kindling,
strings burst on cellos and violins,

woodwind and brass
mangled.

Play your Beethoven now,
barbarians!

But the cruelest thing
I ever saw was
a captured soldier's
copy of Rilke taken and
propped against a tree
to use for target practice.
Every poem reduced to confetti
as he watched
each shot,
his face dropping lower
and lower.

Rain to Snow

As I surrounded your graying face
in my hands to say farewell
I looked up see the rain
convert it self to snow
as if to validate your passing

homebound from the hospice
I skidded into a ditch
and pounded the steering wheel
shouting to no one
"Wasn't it enough that I lost my brother?"

waiting to be towed
soft accumulations of
flakes bore me to a muted
darkness and
I came to understand that you my brother
never stood a chance with father

everything to you was Herculean
eventually you broke
for lack of his softer words
and instead you chased his approval
even in the decades after he died

yet father told me years ago
how he admired you for all you'd done
so maybe you were loved
in some flawed way by him after all

And maybe there is no chance of purity
so much of love gotten or given
is refracted like a sunset wounding the sky

is kept in a reticence

is suffocated in parsimony
leaving us with our hungry places

Between the Longing and the Real

Raise a glass to that which did not come to be.
Here's to arms that never held.
To lips never having kissed
wispy baby scented hair.
Take a deep drought to breasts
that remained unpurposed and
smash the crockery to bits
to this the biggest non event
of all your days.
You've kept it in the quiet too long.

And so late in our years
-our faculties diminished-
I search the house for you
on a predawn winter's morning;
(a morning that holds its
breath in some portent of snow)
only to find you in the garden
-cooing to a carefully cradled emptiness-
until a flake alights on your cheek
and you drop your arms to your sides
and let yourself absorb everything.
It is then I know you've lost your place
between the longing and the real.

The Migratory Habits of Dreams in Late Autumn

During the first cycle you may visit your childhood home
and they will all be there as though still alive
and there may be steaming pots
on the stove and your mother will turn to you and smile
and you will sit in a chair too big for you
while your dog settles his head in your lap

during your second cycle you dream of leaves
that have loosed themselves and drift and tumble
in quiet descent and with each you
give them the names of those who have passed
and whisper sweet prayers as your rake
gathers great drifts of them to a burn pile,
their smoky incense carried up to intersect
with a flock of birds

and in the final cycle
your breathing will slow and lengthen
as your breast heaves and settles
again ever slower and someone will read to you
as you feel the press of their weight on the bed
they will read soft words from a children's book
word by word by word
and pages will rustle like leaves
and there will be no need of anything
—all is said and done—
and you will be loosed
to rise and fall at the same time
as the earth recedes

you drift higher and are carried South
while a snow accumulates and whitens
everything below

Whistling Rachmaninov

Father of my father
our lives never overlapped
as our two hands might have
you died in a train yard
the same year as Rachmaninov
father of my father.

I secreted scraps of information about you
that fell from my parents' conversation
like confetti
father of my father.

Time's music has danced me on
father of my father
should my life share it's last days
with the first of a little one
I will think on what strands of you he carries
and maybe he'll alert to the cry of a train
that will sound a note like "Vocalaise"
and I will whistle the rest as I hold him and
he quiets into sleep
and then I'll whisper
"I am the father of your father."

The Dimensions of Your Soul

Your body ate itself in your final days
temples hollowed as
food diverted to your lungs
the doctor said it's like drowning
--shallow panicked breaths--
morphine pumps to soothe your passage
administered by your children
I kissed your forehead
and told you I loved you
hoping it would get past the drug haze
so you'd take my feeble expression
with you

Then I drove to open spaces
and followed a braiding of clouds
at the far edge of the lake
that made me think of your spine
when I washed your back a week before
each knot of clouds
your vertebrae
I watched you join the sweep of sky
as it made its procession North
to a dark unpeopled land
elk herds migrating across starlit tundra
and you there in all of it
I spoke to the moon that took your face
and the constellations that outlined you
and this time I felt like you could hear me…

Places I Have Known

Of this place
I wish to remember everything
the green out cropped islands
left to wildness
stony ruins jutting over the thin division
of land and sky
with light diffused in gathered clouds
from a low sun

Hamlets less claimed by civilization
 the inflection of words;
and the staccato of foreign tongues
in teeming streets;
bridges trolled by the unwashed
for another coin in their cup

We still hear the music rise
to our open window in the night
to carry away our sleep
as we unravel a mournful dirge
from this lands brutal past

of you my love
I know vast tracks
I've known your taste
when need was everything
the slope of your shoulder
and the measure of your taken hand
the uptilt of your chin

just before you speak

and the topography
of your ear as you tuck a wisp of hair behind it

yet I may catch you
in an unguarded moment
after clearing dinner plates
and I can see the wine
has carried you
to archipelagos of darker thought
that are foreign to me where
I dare not take
my clumsy step
so I touch your cheek
and then you flash a smile
to say you've returned

Wordplay with Rock

There was the summer
I harvested rocks from the beach.
Sand pumiced my feet
and the water painfully cold.

There was the day
my boy came home
(the one I used to rock to sleep)
after all those years
only to take a hit and unravel everything
and all I could do was watch.

...and at season's end
 I drank coffee
under unleafing trees
weighted yet spectral
with stars piercing down.

I wondered how it works with rock.
Does it crackle
when you flame the butane
into the bowl?
Does the euphoria
slam into you
exactly eight seconds
after you suck it into your lungs?

After eight years
did you get back
that righteous high

or are you chasing it still?
And will you keep chasing it
until you are under a rock?

Did you think
I didn't goddamn care?

Your Red Hair

I hear people often die
with the television blaring
maybe half way through
the 10 PM news
like when you were about to be born
and the man on Channel 6
led a group through exercises
as I tried to read a biography
of Georgia O'Keeffe
and I thought
how does this happen—this program that seems to
trivialize your birth?
and I don't recall one word from
that book
but when I saw you the very first time
and the nurse told me your hair was red
I was carried on some updraft of purity
and I forgot about the man doing leg lifts
and the artist who painted
flowers so big
they could almost contain
all my joy

Another Old Man Full Of Stories

There is no danger in that craggy stubbled face
but if you do not dance away discreetly
you'll be subjected to some retelling
—words that curve and snake through memories—
and you'll think "I have no time for this"
and shift to the other foot
it will be a story like a river
run back

it will run like a river through stars
constellations of stories
stories that that flow through the night sky
lighting brilliantly for an instant
filaments of stories woven in the torn fabric of his
memories

stories that are transfusions of the past
vital organs of this old soul
transubstantiated from words
reimagined
softened
a little altered
—does it mattered?—
they course from a weakened heart
they breathe from congested lungs
and emerge from some misfiring of the mind

so let him trap you
-the old man-
as he taps you on the arm to punctuate
a sentence
--are you with him?—
"Have you heard this one before?"

and when you think again he has all the time in the world
you search those watery blue eyes that betray a hint of desperation
and know he may be close to complete silence
so you take his crooked fingers in your hands
to tell him you'll remember that tale
and maybe he'll be gladdened to know something of his remains

Still Life

Shall we give away our things?
Free the house of all but us ?
We'll share a can of soup
and some crackers
and keep our quiet company;
between spoonfuls.

We are a cubist painting in blue tint
titled "Old Couple Eats Dinner."
We are the dissonant strains of an
symphony tuning up
the discontented dialog
of a theater production.

Once we performed such a dance
whirring and spinning and trailing our garments
along the way.
Can the old still dance a little,
I wonder?

I read
the disintegration
of your smile
after you shift your gaze
from me...

but say nothing
so as not to rupture
something in our time space

continuum.

Let me release my dark birds,
send them skyward this clear night
that gifts us all it stars...

and reach across and shelter
your free hand in mine.

When We Were New

Of late I have come to think of rivers,
like the one that flowed below ground
near the bungalow
and when the city busses
would rumble down Washington Boulevard
how it registered in the seismology
of the waterbed;
tributaries of movement
worked into my dreams.

Of late I have come to think of you there,
the first time
all choreographed
and mingled
and coursing
and swelling;
flowing beneath me.

And later lain and sweated,
window open and the announcer's voice
carried on the summer air
all the way from the ballpark.
you ran your finger along the vein
in the fold of my arm
and in our stillness
the whole world pulsed;
trains thrumming,
a lazy plane overhead
as all things commemorated

in harmony in the afterward
of our communion.

Lower Forms of Life

In my book of the dead
I will take my riches with me

Do not say I will be some insignificant particulate
cast on the waters.

I will transition easily to some higher place of
entitlement.

Do not suppose I will announce my name as a
bullfrog with a gulping twang
In some green scum pond

or

be a flower amongst yellow flowers
A pine needle let go to soften a forest path
Some blinding pulsation across the night sky—
lingering in one child's eyes—then gone
To be nothing

Do not say this

I will ascend to high plains
Where the strata is thin and rarefied

and yet I have shed epidermis here
A fingernail clipping along the way
Clumps of grey left near barbers' chairs

Still I will not be something
Chuffing in the undergrowth
Grunting odd noises

Or lifting a leg

To leave a message
In the leaves
In the leaves in the grass

On the Second Occasion of His Passing

Dreams mine a rich vein
unknown in the day's glow
as last night reported his death
a second time

Dawn's a thin membrane of light
and the sheered moon broods into the morning

I work the pathway alone with my dog
--who is whippet thin--
as he breaks through scrub to rupture my thoughts

We come to a pond with its skein of ice
but I think it has a repository of my dreams
threading through its darker waters

Later I will cast a line into it
when it has melted
and it will look as though I am fishing
but this day is set aside to let loss
hemorrhage into my wakefulness…again

The Complete History of Our First Kiss

The old trees bend protectively around us
as we rest on the park bench in our winter wear
your faltering mind following
the course of the river
that is close and sure and deep

even now I can still find your younger face
and remember the pillowy softness
of your lips when ours first met
when we became love desperados

for now we will make our way to the bookstore by
the famous church
and I will buy for you a neglected volume of stories
that will carry you into the long nights
and when we find a place to take coffee
you will caress the weave of the cover
as I serve your cup with an unsteady hand
and I see there is a little less of you this day

should we weight our overcoat pockets with rocks
and wade into the waters?
it will seem like the most natural thing
we will clutch each other and
let the current spin and dance us as our hats float
free
if they find us washed up on some farther bank
will our lips be blue like something that burned pure
and is death just a river that will take us somewhere
else?

for tonight though I will read to you to quell your
agitations

--words you may still find familiar--

and in not too long a time
when I kiss you again
will you think it's our first?

From My Family to Yours

After my brother was killed in Iraq,
he often loomed in my thoughts
and once I even saw him on my drive home.
standing in a distant field
looking slightly
out of place

Sometimes at 3 a.m. -- when I am a casualty
of broken sleep -- I wrap myself
in his fatigue jacket, light a joint,
and stare into the emptiness of the night.

Over beers while on leave,
he told me he was ordered to fire
on a car that crashed through a checkpoint.

"I think they were
just scared,"
he said.
"The three kids
in the back seat
killed too.
The smallest
with big eyes just
staring at nothing."

After telling me this,
he said,
"Maybe I'll be their retribution."

Keeping You Close

Opposing armies fought
a pitched battle in my head
last night
I woke cotton mouthed
and clouded

I kiss your pillow
in your stead
seeking the merest whiff
of your lilac scent
and shake it to see
if it's kept a dream of yours

Just as well you're gone now
dear as I would have wrecked
your sleep something awful

Trousers rolled I walk
the beach
one foot in the water
curious old fool I am
muttering to your ghost
once so corporeal to me
I weave amongst
children and sunbathers
and when I'm winded
I lean on my cane
to appear to gaze
at the water

funny to suppose
I'm not so much as owed
another breath
but still I hold

all my wantings —
just to take one more coffee
with you would seem like everything
to me now

Finally I come upon a black-feathered shag
moored in the sand
and whisper
"Your mate must call for you too
on wild moon bleached nights
as she deepens in the rookery."

Last Things

Sun and moon and earth
dance their dervish.
Moon blooded and gorged
as earth throws darkness
to her face.

I have taken the light from you
only to try to restore it in my clumsy way,
and this is our step, then
with a shimmy and a shake
and a duck and a weave.

And after the dance
press your face
in my shoulder
and know the soft, holy darkness
with me
as we escort each other
to perfect sleep.

And know that one of us
will wake
sometime hence
without the other
and barter
complete forgiveness
for just a minute more.

And one fine day

even the moon will spin past
and seek her own course
and make less the night

Merely Us

Under a dark bloom of cumulus
Dense concentrations of geese wander the sky
I have not been listening
I have not listened
traded all for a sugar high

There is the shushing of the ice
the waves bring to shore
and the sinewy wisps of steam
that skim the waters in the harbor
just before a west wind takes them
near the burning of the sun

There is the watch of the trees
in their slow deliberateness.
in this season of long nights

It is not the world that ends in fire or ice
merely us

The Distance to the Moon

It's funny how little you know in old age
a craggy face and deep set eyes afford no wisdom

It will snow later and
weather systems register in my broken places

mostly I count losses
when a large moon pulls me out of sleep at some
ungracious hour
mostly what I once knew has lost its importance

I wanted to tell
the young man on the bus I sit across from
breaking into his private listening
and the large woman in line at the food store
who tries to make herself small
I want to tell them
the moon is not as far as you think

in a world is swollen with need
we fight our quiet little wars with the ones we have
loved

I walk into a nor'easter
that wets my face with its sadistic kiss
while airliners unseen overhead search out runways

I am sleep shy and shit stained as
I duck into a diner

Should I say it to those at the counter
huddled over their eggs and coffee
seized in Edward Hopper's yellow light

should I say it to my daughter whom I will call later…
my daughter who will erase my message without listening
because she is angry with me
over some unremembered feud

because maybe this time you'll listen dear one
the moon is not as far as you think

July 10, 1939
(On my parents 80th wedding anniversary)

This is a day set in the amber of memory
...the day that set everything in motion

neither could see the coming war
he only saw the white veil
of this 23 year old he'd take

they did not imagine the four
—a girl and the three boys—
evenly spaced until the last

she only saw his blue eyes behind the glasses
the thickness of his oiled hair

they only heard the old priest
in the bright vestments
who prompted their soft replies
with the candle scent of beeswax
in the church's acoustics
that seemed to swallow their words

she only saw his gleaming car
that would take them to Yellowstone
he only felt their awkwardness
and pretended it was normal
as he loaded their luggage in the trunk

there were no strokes or heart failures
or joblessness that darkened the house   yet
only this scatter of days
in relief against the tapestry of their futures

so when the car radio lost all the signals

he sang Alouetta in the French of French Canadians
and she laughed at the funny sounding words
and she slid across the car seat into his gathering arm
as he glanced at her he could see the flecks of light in her green eyes

and later maybe there was hope in the flecks of light in
the night sky as they leaned against the car
in the motel parking lot
even as she felt irrevocably far from home

and she gripped his arm and said sing
"Red River Valley"
his sweet baritone notes enfolding her
her eyes with such promise

Dmitri I Have No Music for This

How did you find the notes Dmitri
amongst artillery shells or the snare of machine gun fire?
I hear there were frozen corpses in the streets
and nowhere to bury them
while some ate wallpaper paste for lack of food
and when the Stukas screamed down
did you hear the minor chords
and convert them to a melody
for the violins and cellos
for your city who gathered the
starving to hear a starving orchestra
play your creation
while still surrounded

Dmitri I have no music for this
with the whole of mankind besieged
when even the ones you love
may carry the enemy
that will cull the old and the weak
when even a warm embrace is insidious
and we are turned against our own hands

Dmitri I have no music for this
when the hospitals are jammed to bursting
I only hear the congested wheeze
and the fevered delirium
when I look from the window and wonder
if the planet has turned irreparably
and will not turn back

Dmitri I have no music for this

(Dmitri Shostakovich wrote Seventh Sympathy while Stalingrad was under siege by the German Army during the Second World War.)

How She Grieved the Old Piano

The old upright should have been
undone with due reverence
screws backed out carefully
wires laid on carpeting
in the ascendancy of the notes they carried
woods musty with cellar dampness
--once given carefully selected veneers—
unhinged and set down softly
keys that offered *Clare de Lune* and *Pathetique*
— blacks and whites—extracted gently
albeit old now and out of tune

but my father demolished it with rude tools
crowbar and sledge hammer
as wood splintered and pedals loosed
and when the sounding board was finally separated from
its cabinet
the mortally wounded instrument
groaned its last terrible note
as it smashed to the floor
on my mother's foot

it wasn't so much the hitch in her step I noticed after that
as her off key humming had ceased
and I saw this violence had created a hard place in their
marriage
that never got back to tenderness

so after my father passed --as men usually do first--
she found a recording of Vivaldi's *The Four Seasons*
and played it often the rest of her winter years

The Way Station

You can hear it call around 4 a.m.
and if the wind driven rain crackles hard against the windshield
if it shakes the ground as it nears
if the crossing gates descend
with lights flashing as the warning bell clangs
as it heads north
because it always heads north
then you know it has come for someone
as age has ransacked another life

there will be news of it tomorrow
in this little town of no consequence
that someone has gone
far beyond the habitation of others
where night is just a bruise behind moon and stars
and there will be a vast stillness in this place
of forbidding cold until the wind has its say
until it brings the voices of all those known

and maybe this is only a way station
until another return to life

and the length of their days
are now a squalid dream of toil and futility
except for the love given
except for that

Touch

To be old is to dwell in an emptied room
quietly tamping down your desperation
--hours leaking away--
until a vessel in your brain ruptures
and all your words are carried off in a tide of blood

and so in lieu of speech
mother
you gripped my arm to say goodbye
or to say you loved me
or to tell me of some wantings you still held
I'm not sure

there is a place where sky and water intermingle at the
far edge of the sea
though you cannot tell one from the other

and I could not sort out what your touch meant
did you cling to me like a drowning soul?

or did your memory return me to my earliest days
when I had no words
but only knew the stroke of your hand
back when you were far away from the edge of this
horizon

Acknowledgments:

Below is a list of poems originally published ***by Finishing Line Press*** in a volume titled ***From My Family to Yours***:

Night Train to Paris
From Distances in Space I Still See My Brother

Ten Cents

The Migratory Habits of Dreams in Late Autumn

Night Forest

Your Red Hair

Upon the Place Beneath

Still Life

The Rio Grande

When We Were New

Dented Brown Fedora

Remembering Your Repeated Attempts At Living

Kept Things

Everything's A Gun Now

Escanaba River

Some Still Come To Ask

Bone And Memory

Failure To Thrive

In The Place Just Before Sleep

Morning Holds Its Breath

The Spirit Of The Horse

A Father Walks His Daughter Down The Aisle And Gives Her Away

To Family And Friends

Hart Island

Wordplay With Rock

From My Family To Yours

Whistling Rachmaninov

A Father Walks His Daughter Down the Aisle and Gives Her Away

During the course of his life, Gary Beaumier has worked in a dizzying variety of jobs that include garbage collector, gandydancer, tutor, teacher, bookstore manager, psychiatric aide, and study hall supervisor. A high point of his employment experience — the culmination of his intertwined love of teaching and of poetry — was a recent stint teaching poetry at a women's prison. Now retired, Gary has become something of a Lake Michigan beachcomber. He has always loved wooden sailboats and has cobbled together several. He spends a fair portion of every day at the local marina with his beloved Halman, the boat he considers "just exactly what I always wanted." A runner when young, Gary now walks an impressive 5-7 miles a day and cheerfully admits to "compulsive walking disorder."

Of course, Gary also writes poetry. His work has appeared in numerous publications, where it has accumulated a gratifying number of honors. His first book, *From My Family to Yours,* was brought out in 2019 by Finishing Line Press. At present, Gary looks forward with pride and delight to the publication of this new collection, *Dented Brown Fedora.*

When we read Gary Beaumier's poems, we notice not only the rich imagery and clear narrative, but the heart and relationship in each poem. His attention to detail creates short phrases that are almost poems on their own. Beaumier speaks to a love that has both sorrow and joy, pain and tears, and invites the reader into an unexpected intimacy.
- Polly Alice McCann, editor of the publication, *Flying Ketchup Press* T

he tender, alert, searching scenes Gary Beaumier puts into his second volume of poetry, *Dented Brown Fedora,* will make any reader pause, sink back down to ear, eye, skin, drink in every breath, blade, and branch. He holds words in his palms, strokes them. His lines are not just vividly imagined. They have an uncanny ability to become a stethoscope by which we listen in to many hearts and hear how a landscape's heart beats.
- Ed Ruzicka, author of the poetry collection, *Engines of Belief* Gary

Beaumier's poetry is fully conscious and absent of any pretentions. With authentic clarity, his verse draws you in, holds you firmly in the moment, then releases you to reflection.
- Spencer Islo, author of the novel, *Keepers Weepers*

Each of Gary Beaumier's poems stops at just the right place, when I ache to read more and am pressed into imagining the rest. His images are fresh and surprising, simple words that, when put together, say just the right thing, creating little gem-phrases I won't soon forget. That the poems seem effortless is a tribute to the restraint and craft of this poet.
- Barbara M. Joosse, award-winning author of over forty children's books, including *Lulu & Rocky in Milwaukee* and the rest of the *Lulu & Rocky* series

www.ingramcontent.com/pod-product-compliance
Lightning Source LLC
Chambersburg PA
CBHW021328190426
43193CB00040B/719